Cave Story
An Underground Adventure

by Mike Graf

Perfection Learning® CA

Illustrations: Michael A. Aspengren, Kay Ewald

Acknowledgments

It has been a great joy to write this book and explore many caves in the process, but of course, I have had much help.

I particularly want to thank Jeff Fitzwater of the Columbia Cavers for taking me out to caves, sharing his enthusiasm and knowledge, and letting me stay alone in a cave for the being-alone experience.

Paul Bernard not only taught me how to rock climb but also shared his knowledge of proper rope and rappel procedures. Tim Skinner, a former student, was an ideal model for the type of child I portrayed in the story.

And to my 1996–97 4th/5th-grade class:

You were outstanding listeners and you also helped me to critique *Cave Story* and get it to the final version it is in now.

Without any of the above, *Cave Story* would have never made it below the ground...

About the Author

Mike Graf is a self-proclaimed caving fanatic and has visited caves all over the world. When not spelunking, he has taught upper grades in elementary school for ten years, trained teachers in science education, and been a television weathercaster.

Mike is the author of several other educational books including *The Weather Report, National Parks Projects,* and *The World's Best Places.* He is currently working on a California State Park adventure series for children.

Mike lives in northern California where he is the main weathercaster for KRCR-TV in Redding.

Table of Contents

CHAPTER 1

TIM CURLED UP like a baby. He was shivering and cold. He was all alone in the dark.

His headlamp shone a small circle of light around him. He widened the beam. Now he could see the whole lonely world he was in. He narrowed the beam to stare at his footprints. They were the only ones he saw.

Tim lifted his light to the walls. The passages and caverns made him feel lonelier and more scared. There were so many places they could be. How many rooms and tunnels had he crawled through? How much of this **karst** had been changed into mazes? It was like the holes in Swiss cheese. Where should he go next?

Tim remembered his father's words.

"Never leave the group. Never go into another room alone. We must always stay together. And if you ever do get lost, hug a **stalagmite.**"

Tim had hardly listened to his father. He had been staring at the cactus that dotted the hills. At the time, Tim hadn't realized how important those words were. How could he have known that there were more than 20 miles of cave passages beneath him?

Now he couldn't get the words of warning out of his mind. "I can't believe I got lost just going behind a rock," Tim mumbled to himself.

A tear dropped onto Tim's leg. He thought back to when he and his father first geared up. They had put on their long johns, helmets, gloves, and knee pads. Then they had checked their three sources of light—the helmet headlamp, the penlight, and the flashlight.

Tim pulled his flashlight from his pocket. He flicked it on to make sure it was still working. Then he pulled out his secret fourth source of light—his candle and matches. He lit the candle. An eerie glow danced across the cave walls. It gave him the creeps. He quickly blew out the candle.

At the beginning of the trip, Tim had climbed down the entrance hole. Then he had walked through the **twilight zone.** This is awesome! he had thought.

He was by far the fastest **spelunker.** He had wriggled easily through the first part of the cavern. He was the only one who didn't scratch and bump himself on the rocks along the way. The ranger had called that first part "Fat Man's Misery." The story goes that a very heavy man once got stuck there. And he stayed stuck until he lost enough weight to get out.

I didn't get trapped or knock my head once, Tim thought. The adults had whacked their heads on the ever-changing ceiling of the cave.

"You'll get used to looking up and watching out," the ranger had explained. "There are **speleogenic formations** and **speleothems** sticking out all over the place. Watch out for these. If you don't, you'll come out with a bunch of scratches. And an awful headache too."

Thinking of wriggling through "Fat Man's Misery" made Tim laugh. And laughing made him feel better.

By now he'd forgotten the ranger's warning. "If you ever get lost, stay right where you are. Don't move! The more you move, the farther you'll wander from everyone who is looking for you. Caves are like mazes. We have no idea how far the unmapped passages go. Or in how many directions. It's easy to get confused between one room and the next."

Tim didn't recognize anything around him. But he pressed on anyway. He squirmed over boulders. He crawled over piles of rocks. He slid through sand and mud. He tramped through tunnels. The **limestone** had been hollowed out over thousands, perhaps millions, of years.

TWILIGHT ZONE

There are three main parts to a cave: entrance, **twilight zone,** and **dark zone.**

The entrance can be a large opening or a small crack.

If you are inside the cave and you can see without a light, you are in the twilight zone. Temperatures vary in the twilight zone.

Many of the cave's animals and bugs live in the twilight zone. Cave swallows and green plants can live there. Snakes, frogs, and salamanders can live there too. Sometimes ringtail cats, bullfrogs, or raccoons go to this part of a cave in search of food. Pack rats may hide in the rocky folds near a cave entrance. Owls may swoop in looking for rodents. During the winter, harvestmen (daddy longlegs) and crickets can live in the twilight zone.

In the dark zone, there is no light at all. The temperature is constant.

CAVE GEOLOGY

Most caves in the United States are made of limestone. This rock is formed from the decayed remains of underwater plants and animals.

Limestone is a **sedimentary** rock. Ages ago, it settled to the bottom of the ocean. Over time, these rock layers built up as mountains above the water level. The rock formations left behind are called **karst.**

The name *karst* comes from the Yugoslavian word *kars,* which means stone. Karstic rocks are found all over the world. Karstic rock formations show dissolved features. These features, or holes, lead to underground passages.

These limestone rocks and cave passages dissolve easily. Rain and surface water mix with the air, soil, and decaying plants. In doing so, they pick up **carbon dioxide.** This weak acid is like the acid in soda pop. Carbon dioxide easily dissolves limestone over time. It also forms **calcium carbonate.** When rainwater reaches an air-filled cave opening, it loses its carbon dioxide. The calcium carbonate is left behind. It gets deposited on the cave's ceiling, floors, and walls. This is how the cave's formations are created.

Tim searched on. His chest was heaving but he was hopeful. He pulled himself up to peek over the top of a large boulder. He shone his headlamp here and there. The light traveled downward into total blackness. He focused the bright beam in and out. He saw nothing. "Maybe this is the bottomless pit that the ranger talked about," he whispered.

He dropped a rock. It fell in silence. Tim counted for five seconds. Then it thumped onto something below. It rolled and tumbled to a stop. Too far, he thought. He started backing up. As he inched away from the edge, he hit his head against a **stalactite.** He rolled onto the rocks and mud.

DROPPING A ROCK TO TEST THE DEPTH

There is no formula for this. You just drop a rock and listen. If you don't hear anything for a few seconds, the drop-off can be deep and straight. If the rock clatters, the drop-off may be uneven. It could have rocks, boulders, and overhangs.

Never climb down into an unknown chamber. It must be surveyed first. And you must use the proper equipment.

"Ow!" he screamed as he rubbed his head. He adjusted his helmet. It had fallen down over his eyes.

"Ooooww," he repeated to the empty underground world. There was no answer. Not even an echo. In fact, all he heard was the dripping of water and his heart pounding in his chest.

"Ooooww," Tim pleaded one more time. At least his head no longer hurt. But his heart still throbbed. And his leg hurt.

As Tim lay there, a drop of water from a stalactite dripped down. It kissed Tim right on the nose. Then another drop fell—and another.

Tim got up. He decided to take a quick sip of water from his canteen. He knew he shouldn't drink too much water. He didn't know just how long the water would have to last.

CAVE DECORATIONS

All decorations in a cave are called *speleothems*. They form from **calcite**-filled water dripping from above.

Stalactites cling to a cave's ceiling. They are formed by water seeping through cracks in the soil. The water dissolves calcium carbonate. It carries the dissolved calcium carbonate inside the cave. If it drips into an air-filled passage, carbon dioxide is lost to the cave air. This makes the water less acidic. Less acidic water can't hold the calcium carbonate. So the calcium carbonate hardens and forms into a speleothem.

Stalagmites form when water with calcite drops from the ceiling to the cave floor. It may take thousands of years to make a stalagmite.

Here's an easy way to remember the difference. Stalac**tites** hold tight to the ceiling. Stalag**mites** might grow up toward the ceiling.

Soda Straw   Stalactite   Column

Stalagmite

Tim brushed off the filth and muck that covered his hands. He leaned against the wall and sniffed the air. Something unusual was in here. He shone his light on his leg. He saw that his pants were torn above his left knee. A trickle of blood rolled down his leg. It wasn't bad.

He ran his light down his leg to the ground. He checked his footing. Then he saw where the smell came from. Tim scooped up a pile of the stinky, fertile soil. What was it? He looked up. They were bat droppings, or **guano.**

There they were. About a dozen Mexican free-tailed bats hung from the ceiling like small vampires. Tim quickly ducked. He dropped his handful of guano and moved on. Several bats swooped down from the ceiling. They flitted about in the cave's constant night.

BATS AND CAVES

Often misunderstood, bats are helpful. Flying up to 50 miles a night, they eat up to 600 mosquitoes per hour.

Many caves were discovered because of bats. One such cave is Carlsbad Caverns. Someone saw a huge number of bats leaving each evening. Now an amphitheater is provided at the cave's entrance. Visitors can watch the bats fly out at night or return in the morning.

Bat droppings, or *guano,* make a powerful **fertilizer.** Many southern California orange groves were first fertilized with bat guano. It came from the Carlsbad Caverns.

Also, guano is an important part of a cave's **ecosystem.** Beetles, flatworms, and spiders feed on bat guano.

The number of bats at Carlsbad Caverns—and most caves—is shrinking. When people poison insects, they destroy the bats' food supply.

Deep in another part of the cave, a search party was forming. The ranger was making plans with the spelunkers. Their old plans had changed. They had come on a **wild-cave** tour inside Mystery Spring Cave. Now they would search for Tim. The ranger and Tim's father, Richard, paired up. The six other spelunkers also paired up for the search.

"Wherever we go, we go together," warned the ranger. "Stay in pairs. And mark your paths with orange nylon flagging.

CAVE EXPLORATION: MARKING YOUR PATH CORRECTLY

In wild caves, mark main travel routes with survey flagging. This will help keep damaging foot traffic to a thin path.

Use markers or reflecting tape at places where someone could take a wrong turn. Remember to remove all markers on the way out.

Some caves may have mapped trails. A mapped cave trail would show the following types of obstacles.

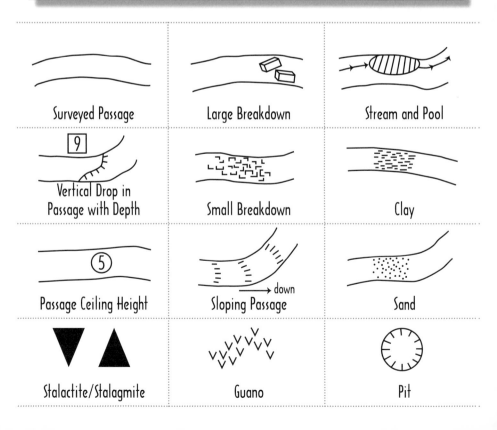

Surveyed Passage	Large Breakdown	Stream and Pool
Vertical Drop in Passage with Depth	Small Breakdown	Clay
Passage Ceiling Height	Sloping Passage	Sand
Stalactite/Stalagmite	Guano	Pit

"Tie it around a rock at spaces within sight of each other. That way you will know how to get back."

The ranger handed a roll of the bright ribbon to each searcher. "I don't want to lose anybody else," he remarked.

Tim's father looked worried. He shook his head. "I don't get it," he said. "He only went around this rock to go to the bathroom."

"Don't worry, we'll find him," another father in the group said. He patted Richard on the back.

They looked around. An endless series of passages, holes, and tunnels surrounded them. And Tim could have taken any one of them.

"Tim," his dad yelled. "Tiiiiimmm!"

CHAPTER 2

"DAAADDD," TIM TRIED again. No reply. He smoothed out a place in the ground. Then he wrote, "Tim was here!"

Tim searched for a rock inside a room. It was the place where he had gotten lost. He wondered now if he would be able to tell when he found it.

He was in a room full of speleothems. Some flowed down the cave's walls like **draperies.** Some were layered on the rocks. They looked like **popcorn** or **cave coral.** Others seemed to have squirted right out of the rocks. They went in all directions.

"**Helictites!**" Tim said. He remembered learning about them. He studied the strange formations up close with his penlight.

"I wonder if I'm the first person to see these?" he whispered. His heart raced with excitement.

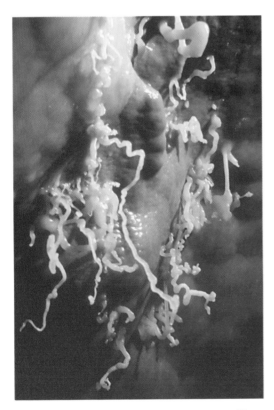

HELICTITES

Helictites are rare cave formations. These unusual shapes seem to defy gravity. They bend, twist, and curl in several directions. There is no pattern to their shapes. The shapes are formed by currents of air.

Helictites are hollow like straws. Tiny bits of water seep through them. The amount of water is so small that it does not form drops. So gravity does not take effect. Water stops at the tip. There it deposits the calcite.

Helictites and shields, Arizona

Above: orange column, Swiss Alps
Right: white draperies, California Sierras

Tim crawled on. He saw a **column** much like one they had seen earlier. The ranger had called it "Eternal Kiss."

The ranger had said, "Notice that this stalactite and this stalagmite are about one half inch apart. It will take about 80 years for them to meet. I hope to be here to see it happen!"

Tim moaned to himself. He longed to see another person. Instead, only cave creatures were listening. Bats, crickets, cave shrimp, fish, and spiders heard him. Maybe the ghosts of early explorers heard him too.

Above the column, Tim saw spiders. About a dozen of them ran for darkness. They were trying to get away from Tim's bright headlamp.

The spiders were huge. They had half-inch, round abdomens!

Tim pushed himself forward quickly. He used his hands and knees. As he moved past the spiders, he let out a sigh of relief. I've never been afraid of spiders before, he thought to himself.

Tim remembered another story the ranger had shared. It had been about the buried explorer in Mammoth Cave. By the time the rangers found him, only his bones were left. The rangers had left his body as a reminder. It was a warning of what can happen to cave explorers.

And then there were the old Indian bones that had been found in a nearby cave. The bones were four to five thousand years old.

"Daaaddd!" Tim called again.

Meanwhile, Tim's father and the ranger had discovered a sort of chute. It was a muddy, slimy waterfall of **flowstone.** It had been created by water dripping underground for thousands of years. It was still moist from the drops above. The water made it smooth and slippery. **Iron oxide** colored it reddish-brown.

The top of the chute looked worn. Had someone recently slid down that way?

They looked closer. They saw boot tracks at the top of the chute. The tracks were about the size of a ten-year-old boy's feet.

"I guess he went down there," Richard said. He explored the darkness with the ranger's powerful searchlight, looking for hand and footholds. How could he get down there himself? He noticed a fresh drop of blood at the top of the chute.

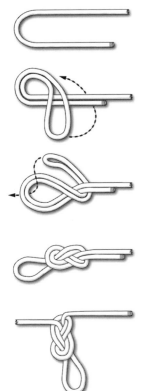

"Looks like we'll need to **rappel** down," the ranger said. "That will be the safest way. We'll use a rope. I'll tie the rope around this rock. Then I'll toss it over the edge. I'll cover it with a rope pad. That will keep it from fraying and breaking. We want to protect our gear. And ourselves," he added.

Richard looked down into the darkness. He knew this was something he'd rather not do. But his son was down there, somewhere.

First the ranger tied a figure eight knot around a rock. Then he tied one back-up knot. "Now it's not going anywhere," he said with confidence.

Next the ranger showed Richard how to **chimney,** or **downclimb.** He pushed his back against the wall. At the same time, he looped his arm through the rope above him. He then held the rope behind his waist. He was down in a second.

Then he started coaching Richard. "Push your backside against the wall. It's your best brake in a narrow cave passage. And look for rocky knobs to grab on to. Hold tight with the rope. Cross your foot over to here. OK?"

"OK," Richard said. But he didn't feel so sure.

Richard started down. He concentrated on each inch. Then about halfway down, he lost it. He was breathing hard. He couldn't move.

"Come on, Richard, you can do it," the ranger coaxed from below.

Richard gathered his courage. I have to think of Tim, he thought. He slowly lifted a foot, groping for the next foothold on the smooth, wet surface. Very carefully, he started lowering himself. Then he made a mistake. He stopped to look below.

Suddenly his footing gave out. He forgot about holding on to the rope. He let go with one hand. SLAP! He fell forward against the rock wall.

"Oooww!" he screamed. He tried to grab on to some rocks. But the rocks pried loose. They tumbled into the darkness below. Richard couldn't hold on any longer. He plunged five feet to the ground.

THE RANGER BENT down to help Richard. "Are you OK?" he asked with worry in his voice.

"Yeah. I'll be fine. Just a few scrapes, I think," Richard replied. He checked for lumps on his forehead.

The ranger helped Richard to his feet. Richard stood up carefully.

Richard didn't have time to worry about himself. "Come on, let's go," he said. "We need to keep looking."

In the distance, Tim heard rocks tumbling. He perked up. He turned toward the sound.

"Daaaddd," he yelled.

"Help!"

"Someone?"

"Anyone?"

But silence was all around him.

Tim wasn't sure whether to move on or stay. He decided to keep moving. He was too nervous to stay in one place.

Tim crept on—into the everlasting night of the cave.

He thought of the desert heat. He thought of the bright sunlight somewhere above him. It was hard to believe. Here it was always a cool, dark, 56 degrees all year long.

Tim groped along the cave's rocky, muddy bottom. His breath poured from his mouth like little clouds.

What he saw next made his heart jump. Others had been here before. Tim read "Jeff Fitzwater, First Expedition—1919." "Fred Chamber's cave." "Smith Expedition—1926." And "Beware!"

Those who had come before had left their marks. They had used candle smoke to burn messages into the cave walls. Creepy, Tim thought. He didn't like thinking about others who had come before him.

Tim crawled farther down the passage. The narrow corkscrew got thinner and thinner. Soon he had to slither along like a snake.

Then a little farther along, he had to take his fanny pack off to squeeze through. He pushed it ahead of him.

The air temperature suddenly got warmer. Tim realized why. He was at a dead end. There was nothing ahead of him except a pile of rocks.

Like the air around him, Tim was trapped. He'd have to come out the way he came in. He felt sleepy. He lay there resting.

Tim thought about another cave tale. Early explorers had lived and traveled in this cave for days at a time. First they had lowered themselves through the cave shaft in guano buckets. Then they had probed the cave's darkness with torches and candles, looking for gold or treasure.

EARLY CAVE EXPLORERS

Cro-Magnon man had explored caves throughout the world, but mostly in Spain and France. These early explorers left behind scratched paint and rock art. They painted with minerals from the cave rocks and the plants outside. Many of their drawings were of animals. Others showed scenes from their daily life.

American Indians also explored caves. They found minerals and salts there. They used them for medicines or ceremonies.

An Indian "mummy" is preserved in Mammoth Cave. It was discovered in 1875. The cave's atmosphere had dried up the body.

More recently, explorers have entered caves by primitive ladders. Or they have lowered themselves in guano buckets. Often these explorers only carried torches or candle lanterns. And sometimes they burnt messages onto cave walls.

Often cave explorers were drawn to the cave by large numbers of bats flying out. One such explorer was Jim White at Carlsbad Caverns. He described dramatic underground scenes. At first, many people didn't believe him. Then Carlsbad Caverns was photographed.

Above: Jim White

Left: In the 1920s, sightseers rode guano buckets 170 feet down into Carlsbad Caverns.

Photos: National Park Service

"I wish I had a torch now," Tim thought aloud. He imagined himself lighting signal fires. He would feel more sure of himself. He would march through the cave with his own torch. His dad would find him safe and happy in his new underground home. Maybe he wouldn't even want to be rescued.

But Tim's fantasy didn't last. Had he fallen asleep? He wondered how long he'd been in here alone. Alone? Alone! Was it hours? Days? Weeks? Was he going to starve? What would his mom think? Would she even know what happened? What about his dad?

"Daaaadddd!" he yelled frantically.

Tim started feeling **claustrophobic.** Panic set in. He tried to turn around but there wasn't room. It was too tight and narrow.

"Calm down," he told himself. He took a few deep breaths. Then he slid backwards using his hands and knees. He slid like a crab scooting away from danger. At last, he could sit up and spin around.

Tim turned off his headlamp to save batteries. He held his hand right in front of his eyes. He couldn't see a thing. It was pitch black. He waited 30 seconds for his eyes to adjust. But it was still pitch black. It was even darker than his bedroom closet!

A drop of water fell. It plunked Tim on the forehead. He could feel the dampness inside the cave.

Tim sat and listened to himself breathe. He was breathing much faster than normal. He was afraid he was having an asthma attack.

Tim took a granola bar from his fanny pack. He peeled off the wrapper and started chewing. Should he be leaving a trail of food like Hansel and Gretel? he wondered. But he was too hungry.

Tim quickly munched the last bits of the bar. The food gave him energy. It renewed his desire to search on. He dropped the wrapper to the ground in hope.

CAVE DAMAGE

Every cave visitor leaves something behind. Even when they don't mean to. They leave lint from their clothes. The lint discolors and damages caves.

Each person may only leave a few pieces of lint. But with thousands of visitors every year, this adds up.

Caves like Carlsbad Caverns have volunteers to help remove the lint. They use brushes, tweezers, and feather dusters along the main trail. They clean the cave to return it to its natural state.

In one year, the clean-up crew collected 27 pounds of lint from the main trail area of Carlsbad Caverns.

If left alone, lint can dissolve parts of the cave! Also, insects will come into the cave just to eat clothing fibers.

Some cave experts are thinking of going high tech. They may install air brushes or vacuums at the cave entrance. This will help reduce each visitor's deposit of lint.

CHAPTER 4

TIM TURNED HIS light on again. Up ahead he saw a passageway. It was like a three-foot tube.

Tim thrust his body forward. He felt scrunched. Half his body was through the **squeeze.** But his feet dangled behind.

He knew he could always go back. But what if he got stuck? he thought.

Tim started breathing faster. His arms felt trapped, pinned against his sides. He couldn't move. This was it, he thought. This was where he was going to die.

But he wasn't ready to give up. He thrust forward again. He pushed as hard as he could. "Ouch!" he cried. He had scratched his cheeks on some cave coral.

But it was working. He was inching through. Now he could move his hands and feet again. At last, he pushed himself out!

The new room he had entered felt a bit cooler. It even felt a bit breezy. Tim wormed his way over a pile of rocks. He saw a beautiful ceiling. It was decorated with more helictites, popcorn, and draperies.

Tim ran his hand along the side wall of wet flowstone. He knew he wasn't supposed to. He knew the oils on his skin could damage the cave. They could change the formations in this part of the cave forever. But Tim was too worried to care.

HOW TO GET THROUGH A "SQUEEZE"

Go down a squeeze feet first. This is very important with a newly explored area. That way, you will be able to push up and climb out.

To climb a squeeze, place your hands under you. That way you can push up from below. It will give you more strength than pulling.

What if the squeeze is too narrow for your body? Try placing your right hand over your head. Place your left hand at your back. This will make you as narrow as possible. This also allows one hand to pull and one to push.

CAVE AIR

Often, wind drafts tell where a cave is. The drafts come up through cracks in the ground. These gusts of wind are caused by varying air pressure. Strong gusts can mean there is a deep cave.

At Carlsbad Caverns, changes occur during winter months. The air pressure in a cold front will differ from the air pressure in the cave. So a cold front can cause more air flow.

Air generally flows into a cave at sunset. It flows out at sunrise.

A change in a cave's **barometric pressure** can affect many things. It can affect the air's movement, humidity, or dew point. It can even cause a "cave rain" or mist.

Heat can enter a cave in four ways: overlying rock, underlying rock, airflow, and water flow. But cave temperature changes are never drastic. In many cases, they hardly change at all.

A cave's temperature is usually about the same as the temperature of the rock. And the rock temperature is about the same as the average annual temperature above ground. Cave temperatures can vary a little between the entrance and deep inside the cave. This temperature variation can cause wind in the cave.

Bad air can gather in lower parts of a vertical cave. Bad air has a high percentage of carbon dioxide. A wild caver can tell the air is bad because it will seem heavy and stale. If you are wild caving in a vertical cave, you should test the air every 20 feet. This will assure that you aren't climbing into a pit of bad air.

Light a lighter to test the air. If the flame is normal, you are not in bad air. If there is a gap between the lighter and the base of the flame, you are in carbon dioxide-rich air. The gap could be quite large—four inches or more. Even worse, the lighter may not light.

If you are in bad air, you might feel hot. Or you may have a headache or unclear thoughts. The best thing to do is climb back up.

Tim studied the walls closely. There were big holes in the rocks. The acid from water had eaten through the limestone. The karstic rock looked just like the ranger had described it.

"I'm standing in a room of Swiss cheese!" Tim told himself.

He laughed. "I'm so hungry, I could take a big bite."

Ahead Tim saw a small **grotto**—a cave inside a cave. It was full of tiny stalactites and stalagmites. It looked like a place where gnomes and other little people might live. Tim wondered if one would pop out. A shiver of fear ran through him.

Tim sat down and stared into the grotto. Maybe a little person wouldn't be that bad. He could sure use the company.

Tim focused his headlamp into the hole. Maybe gnomes weren't that scary, he thought. Maybe one of them would know a way out.

Tim sat and stared into this gnome's home. After a few minutes, he pictured a tiny green creature. It came out to greet him.

"Hello, my friend," it smiled eerily. "And how long will you be staying?" it chuckled. It held its little arms out in welcome.

Tim didn't want anything to do with this gnome. The creature seemed to understand. It wobbled back into the grotto.

Tim stood up and backed away from this strange vision, but not too far.

Just in time, he glanced over his shoulder. He turned and looked down. He was on the edge of a wide crack. He shone his light down. How far did it drop off?

Tim saw nothing. He decided it might as well be the center of the earth. He wedged himself safely against a wall. He stood there. His heart raced.

Meanwhile, Tim's father and the ranger stood at the bottom of the chute. They left the rope for their climb back up. They flagged their path.

Before the ranger would move on, he insisted on checking Richard's injuries. Richard's pants were torn. He was scraped in several places. His cheek was bleeding. But nothing seemed to be broken. So they tended Richard's cuts and bruises and prepared to move on.

They checked their map. They were off the spelunkers' trail. No one had been here before them. Except, maybe Tim.

"Let's try going this way," Richard suggested. He pointed toward an opening in the wall. "If I know Tim, he won't sit still very long. He'll keep moving."

The ranger cut in. "Richard," he said, "we have to find him within the next hour." He pointed to his watch. "Or we'll have to radio above for help. We'll have to get a search and rescue party down here." He paused. "The little bit of food and water he has won't last long."

The ranger didn't want to think about what could happen. It was his tour—a guided spelunking tour. And someone—a ten-year-old boy—was lost.

So many rules had been broken. The boy had left the group to go to the bathroom. He had gone around a corner. But the cave had ten, twenty, or more corners, corridors, passages, and entrances that all looked the same. The boy became lost. He hadn't known which way to turn.

No one had gone with Tim. And he didn't have any equipment. He had no rope, no tape, no nothing!

The ranger was embarrassed. And he was upset. This should never have happened, he moaned to himself. A pit of guilt grew in his stomach. Why hadn't he made the boy stay with them? Or why hadn't he given him something to mark his trail back?

"Tiiiimmm," Richard yelled again. But the rocks absorbed all the sound. Now they too heard the drip, drip, dripping sound of water. It was the sound of emptiness and loneliness.

"Try whooping like this." The ranger showed Richard. "Whoop! Whooooop! That sound travels farther."

They both whooped until they were hoarse. They kept moving, but their hopes had darkened.

CHAPTER 5

TIM'S DAD AND the ranger slid on. Richard ducked to avoid a thin stalactite. It hung from the cave's low ceiling. The stalactite was so thin, it looked like a three-foot-long **soda straw.** "That probably took thirty or forty years to grow," the ranger explained. Several smaller straws hung near it.

"Their growth is slower now," the ranger added. It was as if he were still leading a tour. "That's because of the drier climate above." He stopped himself. This was no time for science.

SODA STRAWS

Soda straws form on the cave ceiling. As water drips slowly, it leaves a small deposit of calcite around the edge of a thin hollow tube. Exposure to the air dries the outside of the tube. The tube slowly grows to the floor. If the tube closes and the water drips quickly, a stalactite forms.

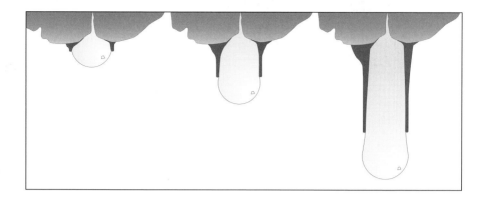

A drop of water splashed Richard on the nose. He looked up. Several wet "straws" hung down. Another one was ready to drip. He looked down. He wondered what kind of formation had started to form under the drips. That's when he saw it.

"Look, it's a plastic bag," Tim's father announced. The ranger picked it up. He stuffed it into his backpack.

"He's been here. He shouldn't be far," the ranger said. "That is, if he stayed still."

Richard half hoped and half worried. He knew Tim hadn't stayed still. He'd probably kept moving.

Richard probed all the nooks and crannies with his high-beam flashlight.

"Tiimmm! Tiimmm! Tiimmm!"

In the draft of the larger room, Tim was cold again. So he sat down and curled up. He hugged himself, trying to keep warm. He rocked back and forth. Just like he used to do in his mother's lap.

He turned his light off. Then he started singing, "I'm lost in a cave. I'm lost in a cave."

He picked up a pebble and threw it into the darkness. It made no sound.

How long had he been in the cave? he wondered. Two hours? Two days? A week?

"Will I ever see the sunlight again? Or colors?" he thought aloud. "What if I die? What if I starve to death?"

Tim stood up. He turned his light back on. He began to walk again. He picked up another rock. He tapped it against the speleogenic formations that were **scalloped** out of the cave's walls.

Each knob that he tapped made a little different sound. He chose two next to each other. He tapped back and forth on the hollow formations. It sounded like music. He was playing his own cave instrument! But, sadly, he was the only person around to hear it.

Tim remembered the tour group. They must be searching for him now, he hoped. That made him feel better.

Tim sat down again. He started playing with the rocks at his feet. He started going over cave rules to pass the time. "Kill nothing but time," he told himself. "Kill nothing but time . . . Take nothing but pictures . . . Pack out what you . . . Leave nothing but . . . Pack out . . ."

Tim squinted his eyes. He tried to study the cave from a different view. The shapes around him seemed to glow and take on life. He saw a Christmas tree! He saw a candlestick! And that one looked like a huge piece of bacon!

Tim wondered if anyone else would ever see the same thing.

FAMOUS AND COLORFUL NAMES IN REAL CAVES

Yes, there are many colorful names of rooms and formations throughout all caves. How exciting it must be to see features like these in caves across the United States.

Angel's Wings	Diamond Cascade	Queen's Chamber
Baby Hippo	Eternal Kiss	Rainbow Lake
Bacon Hall	Fat Man's Misery	Rock of Ages
Bagel Hole	Frozen Niagara	Rock of Gibraltar
Bloody Fingers	Ghost Lake	Santa Claus
Boneyard	Giant Dome	Santa's Frosted Forest
Bottomless Pit	Giant's Coffin	Sherwood Forest
Cakewalk	Giant's Tooth	Snowball Dining Room
Capitol Dome	Grotto of the Gods	Spaghetti Bowl
Cascade Hall	Hornet's Nest	Statue of Liberty
Cheese Factory	The Iceberg	Temple of the Sun
Chinese Meat Market	Iceberg Rock	Three Chessmen
Chinese Wall	King's Palace	Top of the Cross
Chocolate High	L. A. Freeway	Totem Pole
Cracks of Doom	Lion's Cage	The Wedding Bell
Crystal Ballroom	Lion's Tail	Whale's Mouth
Deep Confusion	Moby Dick	Witch's Finger
Devil's Den	Noah's Beard	
Devil's Spring	Oriental Garden	

CAVE WILDLIFE

Trogloxenes are cave visitors. They visit or hibernate in caves. But they usually leave to get food outside. Bats, swallows, cave crickets, and pack rats are trogloxenes.

Troglophiles are cave lovers. They can survive a lifetime in a cave. But they can also live on the surface in cool, dark places. Glowworms, crayfish, springfish, salamanders, spiders, and insects are troglophiles.

Troglobites are highly adapted to cave life. They cannot survive outside caves. Some have lost all color. They are totally white. Some have no eyes. But they have other highly sensitive organs.

They may have long antennas to sense predators and prey. Troglobites tend to be small. They have a low **metabolism** and a longer life span. Eyeless cavefish, crayfish, and salamanders are troglobites. The cavefish are believed to be left from long ago, when caves were underwater.

Tropical caves can have huge cockroaches. Underwater caves might have tube worms, blind cave shrimp, blind cavefish, and crustaceans.

Tim heard water trickling nearby. He slid slowly over to the tiny stream. He dipped his hands in. It felt icy!

He shone his light into the water. There he saw a blind fish, a **troglobite.** The tiny **albino** fish didn't move out of Tim's light. It was totally blind.

Blind white cave crab from Belize.

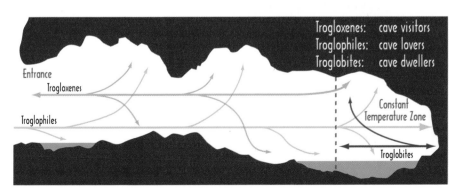

Trogloxenes: cave visitors
Troglophiles: cave lovers
Troglobites: cave dwellers

Entrance
Trogloxenes
Troglophiles
Constant Temperature Zone
Troglobites

I wonder if that's going to happen to me? Tim shuddered. I guess I won't need my eyes anymore.

Tim could hear the water splash through cracks, faults, and underground waterfalls. At times it made sounds like voices.

"Dad," Tim whispered.

"Daaadd!" he yelled. But then he realized it was just water and his imagination. Tim picked up a rock. He flung it angrily.

TIM PICKED UP another rock, a huge one. With as much strength as he could muster, he lifted it with both hands. He hurled it as hard and as far as he could. It crashed against some big boulders. Tim heard it break into pieces. Then it rolled downhill. Finally, it came to rest.

"Did you hear that?" Richard yelled. "Rocks crashing!"
"Tiiiimmm!" he screamed.
"Whoop!"
"Wait," the ranger said. "The sound of rocks banging together carries through rocks by **vibration.** But our voices just get absorbed. Let's try banging rocks."
They found a couple of large stones. They tapped them on rocks and walls. As they tapped, they kept walking. They kept marking their trail with flagging. Every few feet, they would stop and listen.

Tim heard a soft, muffled tapping. The sound echoed through the walls. He perked up. He listened. What direction was the noise coming from?
"Daaaddd!" he yelled. But there was no answer.
"Help!" Tim took another large rock. He hurled it into the darkness.

"There it is again," Tim's dad whispered. He and the ranger looked toward the left. The sound came from a narrow shaft. Would they be able to squeeze through? They had to! They must get to where that sound was coming from.

For a second, Richard thought he saw a light. It was as if a flashlight beam flickered out of that tiny hole.

The ranger squeezed into the passage. It was barely big enough for a boy to crawl through. He squeezed on through the narrow, damp, dusty chamber.

Then Richard tried. He got stuck once. So he undid his fanny pack. And he had to turn sideways. It was a very tight fit.

At last they came out on the other side. They ducked under the decorations on the low ceiling. Then they saw where they were.

They had entered a huge room. It was the size of a whole house!

It was then that they saw Tim's light.

"Tim!" his father yelled, "Tiiiimm . . ."

The light shifted in their direction.

"Dad! I'm over here!"

The headlamp, the searchlight, and the voices now found each other. But there was a span of 50 feet and no direct path between them.

The ranger let out a sigh of relief.

Tim and his father were ready to race toward each other. "Wait there, Tim! Don't move! I'll come get you!" Richard yelled. He dashed up a boulder.

"Wait!" The ranger grabbed Richard's leg just in time. "You don't know what's down there. What's between you and him. There could be cracks, holes, canyons, chasms—anything. We need to go together. And stay together," he added. "We're going to get him safely."

"Don't move, Tim! We're coming!" his dad yelled. He sounded calmer. "OK?"

"OK!" yelled Tim.

RICHARD AND THE ranger probed and searched. They hoped to find a safe path to Tim.

The best way seemed to be across a small pool of water. The pool was about 20 feet wide. It sparkled like a jewel.

"Dad," Tim whispered. He could see the men's reflections through a crack in the wall. "I'm right over here."

"Tim," his dad stared back. "I'll swim over to you!"

"No," the ranger grabbed him. "Look in there!"

Then they looked deep inside the pool. It was a lovely underground lake. It had been formed by a dam of **rimstone.** The lake was filled with sparkling crystals. All around it hung large white **gypsum chandeliers.**

A crystal-like white dust was all around the pool. It was made of **gypsum powder.** Tiny **cave pearls** lay scattered around the rim of the pool. Each sparkled from its own small hole.

RIMSTONE DAMS

Calcium carbonate in water on a gentle sloping floor can build up over time. It can form a rimstone dam.

Pools or lakes form behind the dams. This causes the dams to continue to grow. If the pool dries, the walls are left behind. The dams can also form where water flows quickly. The flow releases carbon dioxide and deposits the calcium carbonate.

CAVE PEARLS

Cave pearls are the rarest of all cave formations. They are smooth, round calcite deposits. They form, like oyster pearls, over a tiny piece of sand or rock. Water passes over the small crater where they lie. It gently rotates and coats the pearl for hundreds of years.

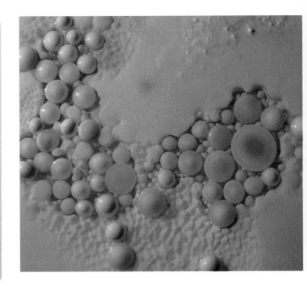

It was as if they had discovered buried treasure. It was breathtaking.

"This is very rare," the ranger explained in a hushed tone. "It's so beautiful. All of the caving world will want to know about this lake. It took thousands, maybe millions of years for these things to form. If we step on any of them, we may ruin them forever.

"But my son," Tim's father pleaded.

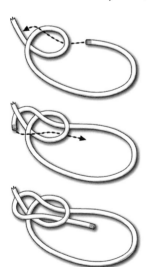

"Don't worry." The ranger touched his forearm. Then he took off his backpack. He opened it up. He pulled out a life preserver. He began to blow it up.

"I knew this would be of use someday," he huffed between breaths. The ranger looped a rope through the preserver. He tied the end of the rope to his waist with a **bowline knot.** Then he tossed it gently across to Tim.

It landed two feet in front of him in the water. Tim reached over and pulled it up.

"Step inside," the ranger coaxed.

42

"Go on, Son," Richard added.

"Put it around your waist," the ranger continued. "Then be as still as you can. Hang on. We'll pull you over. You don't need to swim, paddle, or do anything. We'll just pull you."

Tim quickly put the life preserver over his head. He pulled it down.

Then he carefully slipped into the icy water. He kept his feet up as high and as steady as he could. He didn't want to destroy any of the lake's formations. He had caused enough trouble to this cave, he thought. He didn't want to ruin anything else.

At last, he was on the other side. His dad pulled him out of the water. He held him tightly in his arms. Both Tim and Richard were crying.

"I'm sorry, Dad," Tim moaned.

"It's OK," his dad comforted him. "We found you. It's OK."

After a moment, the ranger added, "You know, we are probably the first people to see this lake. That means we get to name it. And I think that I have the perfect name."

"What's that?" Tim and Richard looked over.

"Lost Boy Lake," the ranger said. "It shall forever be called 'Lost Boy Lake.'" They all laughed and hugged each other tightly.

Appendix

National Park Caves

The following is a list of national parks with caves and their locations. For other open-to-the-public or show caves, contact each state's tourism bureau or the National Caves Association, 4138 Dark Hollow Road, McMinnville, Tennessee 37110, (615) 668-3925.

1. Acadia—Maine
2. Carlsbad Caverns—New Mexico
3. Craters of the Moon—Idaho
4. Jewel Cave—South Dakota
5. Kings Canyon—California
6. Lava Beds—California
7. Mammoth Caves—Kentucky
8. Oregon Caves—Oregon
9. Ozark National Scenic Riverways—Missouri
10. Pinnacles—California
11. Russell Cave—Alabama
12. Crystal Cave, Sequoia National Park—California
13. Timpanogos—Utah
14. Wind Cave—South Dakota

Cave Surveying and Mapping

Early cave explorers tied string from formation to formation to avoid getting lost. Careful records were taken to keep track of how many balls of string were used. It took about nine balls of string to go one mile.

Cave surveying is very difficult work. Modern cave explorers survey caves using a compass, clinometer, and tape measure.

The compass and clinometer determine the direction and slope of the cave's passage. The measuring tape determines length. Surveyors make careful sketches to go along with their measurements.

A clinometer measures vertical angles in caves. It has a dial with marked angles, a level indicator, and a sight. You look through it to view a target site. The instrument then gives you the angle of elevation, or the slope.

Each newly explored passage is also surveyed for historical and biological features, the nature of passages, and hazards. Temperature, humidity, water quality, and samples of cave life may be gathered.

Cave mapping takes patience, skill, and precision. Heights, lengths, directions, and obstacles must be carefully recorded with symbols.

Cave routes are mapped for future cavers. A map helps cavers determine how difficult the cave is. It helps rescuers in emergencies. And a map alerts cavers to a cave's natural wonders or dangers.

Longest Caves in the United States

The following is a list of the longest caves in the United States as of April 6, 1996. This list must be dated because cave surveying and cave mapping are going on all the time.

Mammoth Cave is mapped as the world's longest cave. It has over 350 miles of mapped passages. According to geologists, there could someday be up to 600 miles of mapped passages in Mammoth Cave.

Lengths are given in miles.

1.	Mammoth Cave System—Kentucky	350.000
2.	Jewel Cave—South Dakota	105.820
3.	Lechuguilla Cave—New Mexico	89.350
4.	Wind Cave—South Dakota	78.190

5.	Fisher Ridge Cave System—Kentucky	78.000
6.	Friars Hole Cave System—West Virginia	43.494
7.	Organ Cave System—West Virginia	39.500
8.	Kazumura-Olaa Cave System—Hawaii	37.282
9.	Blue Spring Cave—Tennessee	31.900
10.	Carlsbad Caverns—New Mexico	30.870
11.	Crevice Cave—Missouri	28.201
12.	Cumberland Caverns—Tennessee	27.616
13.	Sloans Valley System—Kentucky	24.630
14.	Xanadu Cave System—Tennessee	23.799
15.	The Hole (Bogga Cave)—West Virginia	23.003
16.	Whigspistle Cave (MCNP)—Kentucky	22.500
17.	Scott Hollow Cave—West Virginia	22.000
18.	Culverson Creek System—West Virginia	20.820
19.	Binkleys Cave System—Indiana	20.060
20.	Blue Spring Cave—Indiana	20.040
21.	Hidden River System—Kentucky	19.884
22.	Honey Creek Cave—Texas	19.188
23.	Windymouth (Wind) Cave—West Virginia	18.000
24.	Butler-Sinking Creek System—Virginia	17.220
25.	Thornhill Cave—Kentucky	16.730

Deepest Caves in the United States

The following is a list of the deepest caves in the United States as of April 6, 1996. Depths are given in feet.

1.	Kazumura-Olaa Cave System—Hawaii	3,609
2.	Lechuguilla Cave—New Mexico	1,568
3.	Columbine Crawl Cave—Wyoming	1,550
4.	Great EX Cave—Wyoming	1,408
5.	Bigfoot Cave—California	1,205
6.	Neffs Canyon Cave—Utah	1,165
7.	Ellisons Cave—Georgia	1,063
8.	Silvertip Cave System—Montana	1,052

9.	Carlsbad Caverns—New Mexico	1,037
10.	Nielsons Well (cave)—Utah	880
11.	Na One Pit (Pit 6083)—Hawaii	862
12.	Big Brush Cave—Utah	858
13.	Papoose Cave—Idaho	825
14.	Meander Belt Cave—Montana	807
15.	Sunray Cave—Montana	804
16.	Bull Cave—Tennessee	741
17.	Lost Creek Siphon—Montana	730
18.	Virgin Cave—New Mexico	723
19.	Chestnut Ridge Cave System—Virginia	722
20.	Spanish Cave—Colorado	711
21.	Ape Cave—Washington	689
22.	Simmons Mingo-My Cave System—West Virginia	683
23.	Dorton Knob Smoke Hole—Tennessee	660
24.	Wind Cave—South Dakota	649
25.	Fossil Mountain Ice Cave-Wind—Wyoming	644

Wild-Caving Trips

Preparing for Wild-Caving Trips

Exploring a show cave requires little more than good shoes, strong legs, and warm clothing. Show caves are commercially developed.

Wild caves require more. Careful planning and preparation are the keys to a safe wild-caving trip. Many factors go into planning a trip. However, with experience, the planning will become second nature.

The following are some tips for planning a safe wild-caving trip.

1. Know your group's experience level, medical problems, fitness level, and so on. A minimum group size is three people.

2. Make sure everyone has the proper safety equipment. Also make sure that it's in good condition. Don't skimp.
3. Tell a responsible person exactly where you are going and when you plan to return. That person should know who to call if you are late.
4. Know your limits. Don't try to explore a cave that is too difficult for your group. An injury or equipment problem becomes more serious the deeper you go.
5. Remind the members of your group to practice cave conservation. They should know how to act and how to take care of caves. Otherwise, they shouldn't be in a cave.
6. Plan ahead. Be prepared for emergencies. What would you do if the group became lost, injured, trapped by flood, and so on?
7. Know your cave. Make sure you know the hazards of the cave you are planning to explore. Some caves have bad air. Some are prone to floods. Some have bats. Others have areas of loose rock. Plan to avoid those areas. Or avoid those caves.
8. It is very important that you have permission to enter someone's cave. If you can't find the landowner or if he or she does not want you to enter, go to another cave.

Recommended Equipment List

For a safe wild-caving trip, each person should have the following.

- strong, durable, fast-drying clothing. Polypropylene is a good choice. It will keep your body warm and dry. You may be able to wear T-shirts and jeans as long as you have knee and elbow pads.
- white-soled, ankle-high boots with good traction. Black-soled boots may stain the cave.
- a good quality rock-climbing helmet

- at least three light sources. The main light source is on the helmet. The other two light sources can be flashlights. You can also bring a small candle. The helmet lamp can be electric-, battery-, carbide-, or flame-powered. Carbide is a chemical that combines with water to produce a gas. Carbide lamps cannot be used near large sulfur deposits. A fire could occur. Batteries are heavy. Also, the light from a battery is duller. Carbide lamps are bright. They can produce heat too. Heat may be needed if someone becomes lost or trapped. But they can also burn a person. Carry a repair kit for a carbide lamp. Carry extra batteries for an electric light.
- a first-aid kit that includes the following: tape, gauze, betadine surgical scrub, aspirin or nonaspirin painkiller, notepaper, and a pencil
- an adequate amount of high-energy food, depending on how long you'll be in the cave
- plenty of drinking water. If the cave has good water, you can carry a water filter.
- a wool or synthetic hat
- emergency telephone numbers in your helmet

Each group should carry the following items.

- a dry clothing article such as a wool sweater
- a short, static caving rope
- a heat tent (or a minimum of two foil space blankets)
- a heat source such as a carbide lamp with carbide and water, a candle lantern with candles, long-burning candles, or a small stove with fuel
- a repair kit to fix any equipment you carry
- a watch
- a map of the cave (if possible)

The following items are optional.

- gloves and knee pads

- a knife
- additional food and water
- vertical gear. You would need to be trained in single rope methods to use vertical gear.
- SCUBA diving gear: a wet suit, tank of compressed air, mask, and other special gear. Some caves are completely underwater. To explore them, you would need to be a trained SCUBA diver with additional training in cave diving. There are special dangers in an underwater cave. If you run into problems, you can't just surface to get air.
- a sketch pad for drawing formations
- a 100-foot measuring tape
- a camp stove and freeze-dried food for longer trips
- a rugged, durable backpack that allows you to push, drag, or fanny pack it, or tie it to your ankle

Remember—you must carry everything out of the cave!

Where Are the Wild Caves?

You may be able to go wild caving in a show cave. Some show caves have special wild-caving tours.

Local caving clubs know where wild caves are. They generally like to keep their locations secret, however. When fewer people know about the caves, it is more likely that they will be left unspoiled. The best way to go wild caving is to contact your local caving club. For that address, write to

National Speleological Society
Cave Avenue
Huntsville, AL 35810

Wild-Cave Rules and Etiquette

Some wild caves, like Lechuguilla in New Mexico, are closed to the public. They are used only by experienced cavers doing scientific explorations. Respect their use.

When exploring any wild cave you should

- remove all trash and human waste.
- wear nonmarking boots. Some areas prefer that you wear no boots to prevent damaging flowstones.
- never break a stalactite off for a souvenir. You'll ruin the formation in a second. Cave formations can take thousands of years to form.
- never toss coins. They can stain pools.
- respect the water. Keep it clean. Caves are connected to underground water supplies.
- make sure that the next visitor can have as wonderful an experience as you had. So leave caves exactly as you found them. Follow these general rules.

Take only pictures.
Kill nothing but time.
Leave nothing—not even footprints.

Glossary

albino   organism that has no pigment, or color

barometric pressure   the pressure of the atmosphere. In weather forecasting, a rising barometer means fair weather. A falling barometer means stormy weather.

bowline knot   a knot that neither slips nor jams. Used by cavers and climbers.

calcite   calcium carbonate that has crystallized. Includes limestone, chalk, and marble.

calcium carbonate   compound found in nature in calcite, plant ashes, bones, and shells. It is used in making lime and cement.

carbon dioxide   a colorless gas that is used by plants in photosynthesis and given off by animals in breathing

cave coral   forms where water evaporates, leaving behind calcite deposits. Also called popcorn.

cave pearls   smooth, round calcite deposits. They form, like oyster pearls, over a tiny piece of sand or rock. Water passes over the small crater where they lie, gently rotating and coating the pearl for hundreds of years.

chimney/ downclimb   to push one's back against the wall while looping an arm through the rope above, then behind the waist

claustrophobia   fear of being in a narrow space

column   formed when stalactites and stalagmites come together

dark zone	area of a cave where no daylight comes in
draperies	form along cracks on a sloping ceiling. Because of certain minerals, they are often translucent. Iron tints them brown and orange, making them look like bacon.

National Park Service

ecosystem	an environment and the organisms within it that function as a community in nature
fertilizer	a substance used to make soil richer
flowstone	forms when calcite-filled water streams over rocks for ages, leaving an icing-like coating
grotto	cave or recess in a cave
guano	substance, such as bat excrement, used as a fertilizer
gypsum chandeliers	stalactite formation made of hydrous calcium sulfate. They can be 20 feet long.
gypsum powder	fine white powder made of hydrous calcium sulfate
helictites	rare cave formations. These unusual shapes seem to defy gravity. They bend, twist, and curl in several directions. There is no pattern to their shapes. Like straws, they are hollow. Tiny bits of water seep through them. The amount of water is so small that it does not form drops. So gravity does not take effect. Water stops at the tip. There it deposits the calcite. The shapes are formed by currents of air.

iron oxide	a compound of oxygen and iron. Has a reddish color.
karst	an area or region made of limestone—with sinks, caverns, etc.
limestone	formed from the decayed remains of underwater plants and animals. Limestone is a sedimentary rock.
metabolism	the rate at which a living thing uses energy
popcorn	it forms where water evaporates, leaving behind calcite deposits. Also called cave coral.
rappel	to climb or slide down a rope in a certain way that gives the climber control over speed and distance
rimstone	formed by calcium carbonate in a water solution on a sloping floor. Builds up over time.
scalloped	shaped like the shell of a scallop
sedimentary	rock that ages ago settled to the bottom of the ocean
soda straw	forms on a cave ceiling. As water drips slowly, it leaves a small deposit of calcite around the edge of a thin, hollow tube. Exposure to the air dries the outside of the tube. The tube slowly grows to the floor.
speleogenic formation	formation or shape in a cave
speleothems	all cave decorations. They are formed from calcite-filled water dripping from above.

spelunker	someone who explores and studies caves
squeeze	a narrow passageway
stalactite	clings to a cave's ceiling. It is formed by water seeping through cracks in the soil. The water dissolves calcium carbonate. It carries the calcite inside the cave where, over time, the drips form a stalactite.
stalagmite	forms when water with calcite drops from the ceiling to the cave floor. It may take thousands of years to make a stalagmite.
troglobites	animals that are highly adapted to cave life. They live in complete darkness and never leave the cave.
troglophiles	animals that can survive a lifetime in a cave. They can also live aboveground in cool, dark places.
trogloxenes	cave visitors such as bats and swallows. They visit or hibernate in caves.
twilight zone	area in a cave where you can see without a light source. Many animals live in the twilight zone.
vibration	a quivering or trembling motion that carries sound, such as notes from a musical instrument
wild cave	a cave other than a show cave

Index